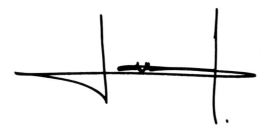

Philip Jodidio

JEAN NOUVEL

1945

Giver of Forms

TASCHEN

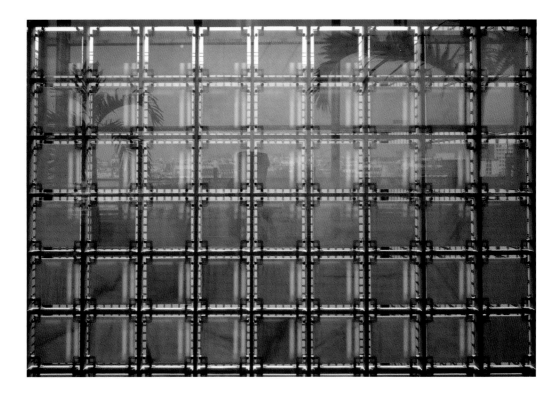

Illustration page 2: Jean Nouvel, 1986,
photograph by Robert Doisneau

Illustration page 4: Institut du Monde Arabe,
Paris, France, 1981–87

© 2012 TASCHEN GmbH
Hohenzollernring 53, D–50672 Köln
www.taschen.com

Editor: Florian Kobler, Cologne
Design: Sense/Net, Andy Disl and
Birgit Eichwede, Cologne
Collaboration: Inga Hallsson, Cologne
Production: Tina Ciborowius, Cologne
Final artwork: Tanja da Silva, Cologne
Translation: Pamela Hargreaves, Paris

ISBN 978-3-8365-3080-4
Printed in Germany

To stay informed about upcoming TASCHEN
titles, please request our magazine at
www.taschen.com/magazine or write to
TASCHEN America, 6671 Sunset Boulevard,
Suite 1508, Los Angeles, CA 90028, USA;
contact-us@taschen.com; Fax: +1 (323) 463-4442.
We will be happy to send you a free copy of
our magazine which is filled with information
about all of our books.

Contents

Introduction

Architect, builder, or dreamer? To create space, a place to live, or to erect a sign in the urban chaos that all is not lost to speculation and the endless repetition of banality? To fit into an existing environment, or to create singularities, signals to those who may understand that some resist the temptations of modern conformity? These are theoretical options for the creative architect, but the pressures on the builder are such that even the strong-willed often bend and agree to play the game. What of style? Some periods have known a dominant style, one that an architect could contradict only at the risk of losing his reputation, and yet some dared precisely that, changing the direction of a profession that in the best of circumstances can become an art. These rare architects are the form givers, those who lead and break the rules, eventually to be understood by their peers and the public at large. Frank Lloyd Wright or Ludwig Mies van der Rohe set out in almost diametrically opposite directions early in the 20th century, and between them gave form to modernity. The style and thought of Wright may have been more difficult to imitate than the geometric rigor of Mies, or even the more lyrical work of Le Corbusier, but between them, these men defined the architecture of their time. Today there is clearly no dominant style, even if computer generated "blobs" or other manifestations of technology seem to have swept over the planet like a plague. When the "new" rhymes with the ephemeral, it may be that there is a thirst for more "genuine" forms that is even greater than in times of a dominant style.

Jean Nouvel is a giver of forms. It may be too early to place him in the pantheon of modern architecture's greatest, but he has displayed a remarkable sense of measure and originality that set him apart from others of his generation. Born in 1945, he is now entering the period of his life when an architect attains recognition. Building, simply put, takes more time than painting or sculpture. And where large sums of money are concerned, clients prefer to trust a known quantity than a young upstart. Beginning with the Institut du Monde Arabe in Paris (1987, with Architecture Studio), the Fondation Cartier (Paris, 1994), and more recently the Lucerne Culture and Congress Center (2000), the Nantes Law Courts (2000), or the Agbar Tower (Barcelona, 2005), Nouvel has moved beyond the phase of local celebrity to join the ranks of architecture's small club of international "stars," designing a tower in Tokyo or a museum in Rio, cutting a familiar figure with his black hat and tough look. Born perhaps more of shyness than of hubris, Nouvel's appearance is, of course, of little significance as opposed to his rich and surprising architectural vocabulary. At his best, he walks the fine line between

a powerful gesture and functional design. He is almost never outrageous, though some of his early buildings do flirt with claustrophobic or brutal space.

One of the ways in which Jean Nouvel navigates between the extremes of brutality and sophistication in his architecture is through the refined use of ambiguity. Very often the viewer or user of one of his buildings is taken aback by certain features, and yet reassured by others. There are stairways and windows and they are more or less where they might be expected to be, and yet there is also an astonishing overhanging roof, as is the case in his buildings in Tours or Lucerne, or a scene from a movie on the ceiling of a hotel room (Lucerne). This man who dresses in black is fond of this product of the combined colors of the spectrum, using it in the Lyon Opera or the Nantes Law Courts to great effect. Reflective or opaque, black is symbolic of the unknown, of fundamental ambiguity. So, too, when Nouvel uses architectural-scale glass screens as he does at the Fondation Cartier, or the Quai Branly Museum in Paris, he plays on the ambiguity between façade and interior, between the inside and the outside, between reflections and more substantive realities.

Rebel with a Cause
Jean Nouvel was born in Fumel, a town of 5800 inhabitants located in the Aquitaine region of France. Set in an area fought over by the French and the English in the 14th and 15th centuries, one of its main claims to historic interest is the 16th-century uprising in which residents invaded the castle and killed the Baron of Fumel. Known for its forges since the 15th century due to local ore deposits, the town long relied on paper and metal production for its livelihood, before converting in more recent years to tourism, based on the attraction of the neighboring castle of Bonaguil.

Nouvel at first wanted to be a painter, but he entered the École des Beaux-Arts in Bordeaux in architecture in 1964. He moved to Paris the following year and was admitted to the École nationale supérieure des Beaux-Arts, obtaining the highest grade on the entrance exam in 1966. From 1967 to 1970, he worked in the office of Claude Par-

Dick House, Saint-André-les-Vergers, France, 1976–78
Local authorities required changes in the structure, which the architect added in red br

ent, theoretician of the "oblique" and one of France's more influential architects. In 1970, Nouvel created his first office in collaboration with François Seigneur, an architect strongly inclined to artistic interventions in the built environment. He obtained his degree (DPLG) in 1972, but, a year before that, he was named the architect of the Biennale de Paris art exhibition. In 1980, Jean Nouvel enlarged the Biennale to formally include an architecture section. From the earliest phase of his career, he was consistently involved in debates and dissent concerning architecture in the urban environment. Co-founder of the "Mars 1976" (March 1976) movement and of the Syndicat de l'Architecture (Architecture Union) in 1977, he was an instigator of a "counter-competition" to try to improve the fate of the Paris Halles area, the former markets razed to make way for dubious green space and an unfortunate Piranesian underground shopping center.

Nouvel's first significant built work is the Maison Dick (Saint-André-les-Vergers, 1976–78). Nouvel calls this house an example of "critical architecture" because his original project was rejected by the local administration. He responded not by abandoning the design, but by asking that the administration "correct" his original concept. Accepting this act of censure, Nouvel turned the process into a visible commentary on what was being asked of him, by allowing an echo of the originally planned arches to appear in brown brick between the "imposed" red brick surfaces. It might be recalled that Nouvel had his schooling in Paris at the time of the 1968 student uprisings that led to significant change in the French educational system. Even in this early example of revolt, he invites the administrative authority to carry out its hidden desire to censor, while making his final design an implicit criticism of the imposed aesthetic.

The clinic designed by Jean Nouvel for Bezons, in the Val d'Oise near Paris, was, in a different sense, also an act of revolt. In this rather bleak place, the architect chose to clad an essentially ordinary concrete structure with an aluminum skin and details like portholes that brought to mind a ship more than a medical facility. Nouvel is, of course, not alone in the modern era in giving a building a maritime theme, but this is some-

how a different ship than one that Le Corbusier or more recently Richard Meier might have designed. It is not the kind of modernism that was meant to float lightly on its surroundings. There is heaviness or a brutality in Nouvel's ship that speaks of the contrast between the hope of sailing to a better location and the unfortunate reality that this building is very much anchored in its site. Not airily optimistic, but surprisingly luminous in its gray background, the Bezons Medical Center begins to define Nouvel's fundamental acceptance that buildings have their location and their roots in the earth. Much of modernism, of course, consisted in the systematic rejection of the weight of architecture, sitting lightly on the land like Corbu's Villa Savoye.

The year 1978 saw Nouvel design what has frequently been described as one of his angriest and most brutal structures, the Anne Frank High School in Antony. Facing an imposed prefabrication system that implied a use of up to 50 repetitive elements, the architect instead reduced his vocabulary to the strictest minimum and made ample use of cinder blocks, zigzagging fluorescent lighting, and a willfully aggressive decorative pattern. Much has been made of the cleverness of architects like Rem Koolhaas who "discovered" industrial materials in the 1990s as though they had invented them. Nouvel here calls on industrial detailing and makes a strong commentary on the misunderstanding of prefabrication that turned so many French and European neighborhoods into ugly, almost completely unlivable environments. He is close to some expressions of contemporary art that also intentionally reject "beauty" as an immediate criteria of judgment. His is a rugged beauty born of the industrial, urban postwar world, and not of the idealistic prewar Bauhaus-influenced *tabula rasa*. Here, as is the case in his later Nemausus housing in Nîmes, his powerful commentary rises above and does not interfere with the intended function of the building. Calculating and distant, the modernist masters often seemed to be unwilling to dirty their hands with the real problems that their methods and designs created. Nouvel, with his typical energy, or even rage, rejects the cookie-cutter mode of architecture, turns the typologies upside down, and still produces a usable and thought-provoking school.

...en's Play Center Les Godets,
..., France, 1980–84
...de, "crayon" colored, the other in raw
...and brown steel.

One of the first indications that Jean Nouvel is able to deal with a great variety of different situations with a high level of originality was his 1980–84 renovation of the Belfort Theater. This 3300-square-meter project involved a 19th-century structure that had been renovated in 1930 and in 1983. Nouvel was called on to work on two foyers, a 700-seat theater, a small 60-seat room, an exhibition area, backstage facilities, offices, and a café-bar. In collaboration with François Seigneur and Jacques Le Marquet for the specifically theater-related questions, the architect chose to open the old structure toward the city and to chop into it in a rather brutal way, leaving rough marks where mediocre restorations and the weaknesses of the original design came under his scrutiny. Contrasting what he describes as the "gold, lacquer, and velvet" of the actual theater with the rough, unfinished look of many walls, Jean Nouvel does here, in a different way, just what he did in the high school in Antony—he accepts as a given the mediocre aspects of the project and builds on them without denying their existence. Although the Maison Dick and the high school were new structures, they both confronted the reality of their situations. Jean Nouvel comments on the architectural reality of the project, but he incorporates a critique that speaks of the history of the structure, and brings it up-to-date without resorting to artificial or "cosmetic" devices. Just as he pioneered the use of industrial detailing in Bezons, Nouvel here is one of the first architects of the time to apply the kind of rough restorations that have become so popular in art exhibition spaces, for example, since the 1990s. Leaving a wall with traces of its real scars, or layers of paint, is a device that numerous others have since adopted, without often acknowledging that Nouvel led the way. Perhaps less expensive than a smoother approach, Nouvel's way of dealing with the Belfort Theater also allows the history of the building to remain present.

Mitterrand's Brave New World of Culture
Though the French have often been critical of the "reign" of President François Mitterrand, which began in 1981, his 14 years in power marked an emphasis on art and architecture that has not been equaled since. Jean Nouvel might be considered the first architect of his generation to have benefited from the large state-financed projects launched by Mitterrand, but he was unsuccessful in his subsequent bids to design the new Ministry of Finance on the banks of the Seine and, at the opposite end of Paris, where a little-known Danish architect was selected to build the symbolic "Tête Défense" building. Nouvel, though favored for the "Grand Louvre" project by Culture Minister Jack Lang, lost that commission to the Chinese-American architect I. M. Pei, who erected his famous Pyramid in the inner courtyard of the palace. But even before what came to be called Mitterrand's "Grands Travaux" got underway, Jean Nouvel did win another job on the Seine, on the Left Bank, within site of the rear of Notre-Dame Cathedral.

Designed in association with Gilbert Lézénès, Pierre Soria, and Architecture Studio, the Institut du Monde Arabe catapulted Jean Nouvel to a new level of fame. Meant to mark the presence of the Arab world in the French capital and to be financed in good part by Muslim countries, the Institut is in many senses an exercise in bridge building. As Nouvel has pointed out, it seeks not only to make reference to Arab design with its *mashrabiya*-inspired decorative window patterns, but also to mediate between its rather undistinguished modern neighbors and the more significant historic monuments in the distance. The challenge was to make a modern statement on an awkwardly shaped but well-placed site while not creating the kind of rejection of the modern that the

French were known to be capable of, especially in such a location. Though recognized by the prestigious Aga Khan Award for Architecture, the Institut du Monde Arabe has relatively few substantive references to the Muslim world—rather, it is a showcase for exhibitions and a library dedicated to Arab subjects. Everything, from the unexpected and narrow path used to enter temporary exhibitions to low ceilings in many places, creates surprise within the structure. Though darkness does characterize some areas, such as those near the elevators, the Institut is more obviously dedicated to the light and the views of Paris afforded by almost every level, right up to the spectacular roof-top restaurant. The sweeping curved quayside façade of the building succeeds at once in announcing the presence of an exceptional building and in following the flow of traffic that comes both from the quay and from the neighboring Boulevard Saint-German. With a higher budget than any building that Nouvel had worked on to that date, the Institut du Monde Arabe is not as much an act of protest or critique as the buildings in Bezons, Antony, or Belfort. It is a subtle and pragmatic solution to a complex set of requirements. With a prestigious site, Nouvel shows here that he is able to orient his talent with great precision in function of the circumstances. The IMA is powerful without overpowering any neighboring structure. It is modern without being offensive, it is a statement for the successful integration of contemporary architecture into even as conservative and historic a city as Paris. Even if the elaborate diaphragm system of the *mashrabiya* windows intended to filter light in different ways according to the time of the day never worked properly, the IMA remains, almost 20 years after its construction, a convincing urban statement.

François Mitterrand's brand of state-sponsored cultural enrichment surely inspired others to encourage art and architecture in France. One of the most noted of these was Jean Bousquet, mayor of the southern town of Nîmes and also head of the Cacharel clothing company. Bousquet called on numerous well-known architects to improve his historic but economically troubled city. While Norman Foster was asked to build a "mediatheque" opposite the Roman "Maison Carrée" in the city center, it fell to Jean

Institut du Monde Arabe, Paris, France, 1981–87
A homage to "great Arabian architecture of geometry and light," with a façade that "programs" the interior through its perforation and shadows.

Nouvel to erect one of his most controversial and innovative projects, the Nemausus housing blocks. The maritime theme already developed by the architect in Bezons here takes on an even more evident presence. The 114 rent-controlled apartments of this complex are located in two distinctly ship-like volumes. Acting in an unexpected way within a set of apparently rigid public housing constraints, much as he did when he took on the high school in Antony, Jean Nouvel chose to make active use of industrial materials for budgetary reasons, which permitted him to increase the size of the apartments by no less than 47 percent as compared to the average for French welfare housing. Working here again with François Seigneur and the French artist Daniel Buren, known for his striped works, Jean Nouvel sought to somewhat soften the harshness engendered by his industrial approach through the insertion of art. It remains that Nemausus is stark both inside and outside. Though he firmly defends his choices in this instance, it is a fact that for reasons beyond the control of the architect, the project cannot be considered a real success. Poor maintenance and the counter-productive decision of the public housing authority to rent the comfortably sized apartments on the basis of the number of square meters (making them prohibitively expensive for low-income clients) have resulted in high turnover rates.

When local authorities complained bitterly that Nemausus might well be a case study in what not to do when building public housing, and suggested that the buildings be torn down, Jean Nouvel responded with a lively exhibition he organized in the context of the 2000 Venice Architecture Biennale. As he has in many cases, Nouvel apparently relished the controversy generated by his buildings and defended himself vigorously even as he devoted space in Venice to explaining the critiques that were directed against him. Objectively it can be said that Nemausus is too harsh, that it relies on industrial materials and bare concrete walls to an extent that is not conducive to the warmth of homes, especially in this southern area of France, which is more used to earthenware tiles than to aluminum staircases and unadorned concrete. But, once again, Jean Nouvel took on this project with the intention of building what was asked of him while breaking as many rules and conventions as possible. For a given budget, why do social welfare apartments necessarily have to be small and unpleasant? Intentionally opening all of the apartments of Nemausus to both sides of the buildings allowing a free flow of air in the warm months, he showed his concern for the comfort of the residents. Lack of maintenance and an aggressive pricing policy surely did more to disenchant potential residents than did Nouvel's aesthetics, but it may be asked if the degree of sophistication he applied to his architectural and artistic choices here really corresponds well to the level of education and aesthetic sense of those called on to live in Nemausus.

Moving Beyond France

Conceived about the same time as the Tours Sans Fins, two of Jean Nouvel's built works confirm his emergence on the center stage of French architecture. The first of these was a task of renovation, albeit a very prestigious one since the site is in the heart of the city of Lyon—on the same square where the city hall and the Palais Saint Pierre (with the Musée des Beaux-Arts) are located. As he did in Belfort, the architect engaged in a dialogue in Lyon with the existing 19th-century theater intended as an opera and dance facility. The most visible intervention of Jean Nouvel is the addition of a very large barrel-vaulted roof with spaces below the vault used for ballet rehearsal and

administration. Clearly working in a more prestigious environment than he did in Belfort, Nouvel manages to triple the floor area of the existing building while retaining its original masonry walls. He does respect the historic architectural environment of Lyon, and yet many features of the opera, from the vault, visible on the city skyline, to the black and rather low entrance foyer, speak an entirely different language—that of a modernity tempered by the bold gestures of Jean Nouvel. Again, many architects might have preferred to build from the ground up, making their own statement. Nouvel's statement is somehow all the more present and strong because he has dared, as he did in Salzburg, not to create the better part of the envelope of his design. The barrel-vaulted roof can be criticized as disproportionate and unrelated to the walls that hold it up, and yet, lit from the inside at night, this distinctive shape becomes a new symbol of the city, and signs of its inner activity make it glow even more. The creation of the Lyon Opera is not the act of an architect bent on imposing his own personal style, and even less an attempt to fit into a fashionable mold. What is personal about it is its audacity, its surprising vitality in the face of an unlikely combination of past and present. A city like Lyon, and indeed most European cities, are in desperate need of the kind of pragmatic solution that Jean Nouvel provides here to the apparent contradiction between past and present, between masonry and glass or steel. He combines and blends the two into an unexpected but efficient solution.

As he did when he worked on the Institut du Monde Arabe, Jean Nouvel has often been called on to build on sites that are significant in terms of their cities. This was the case in Lyon and it is also that of another of his major works of the period, the Tours Conference Center, which is set just opposite the railway station and close to the historic city. Though Tours has a rich architectural tradition, the main dialogue established by Nouvel here is with the station and the square that separates his building from it, and the large avenue that runs opposite the entrance. Called the Da Vinci Conference Center because Tours is not far from the Castle of Ambroise, where the Italian genius died, the most visible feature of the building is the flat, projecting roof. Low,

Endless Tower, Paris-La-Défense, France, 1
The apparent mass of the tower lightens as it rises, creating an almost evanescent presenc the Paris skyline.

sleek, and beetle-like in its form, the center provides for complex variations in its internal functions with auditoriums for 2000, 700, and 350 people, an exhibition level large enough for 120 stands, 800 square meters of meeting rooms, and a restaurant large enough for 800 people. Calling again on his favorite shiny black interior finishes, Nouvel brings surprising gestures—like the suspension on cantilevered beams of two of the auditoriums to this design—but, above all, he demonstrates a rigorous capacity to meet programmatic requirements in an efficient manner. Where he called on nautical themes in Bezons or Nîmes, the Tours structure also may resemble a very modern ship, coming to a halt on this site, much like the rapid TGV trains pull in to the neighboring railway station. The structure is far from static, if only because of the incessant movement implied by an active convention center, but Nouvel's suspended volumes, occasionally claustrophobic spaces, and bold projecting roof all serve to emphasize its impression of continual movement. Sleeker and less industrial in its vocabulary than either Nemausus or the Bezons facility, this is a decidedly contemporary ship, but not one mired in the aggressively ordered grids of modernism. Its inner complexity is smoothly covered over, providing yet another source of surprise for visitors, who are instantly caught up in its inner activity.

Shopping, Art, and More Controversy

The years 1994 and 1995 were rich ones for Jean Nouvel, both in terms of inaugurations, with the opening of the Fondation Cartier in Paris, the Galeries Lafayette in Berlin, and the Euralille shopping center in Lille, and in terms of controversy, in particular over his competition-winning design for the "Grand Stade" intended to host the 1998 Soccer World Cup. The Cartier building, located on the upper part of the Boulevard Raspail in Paris, is an exemplary exercise in mixed-use construction in the French capital. The ground floor and one underground level were intended for the exhibition of contemporary art, collected and displayed at the instigation of Cartier CEO Alain-Dominique Perrin. Most of the rest of the structure was intended for office space, both for the Cartier Foundation and for the international division of the jewelry firm. Located on the site of the former American Center, the Cartier building did not have to deal with a typical Parisian set of historic monuments, but rather with more modern buildings, such as the École Spéciale d'Architecture at 254 Boulevard Raspail. The site of generous size would accommodate a garden as well as the building, but Nouvel created a first architectural surprise by erecting a glass wall just beside the sidewalk of the boulevard. Though designed like the actual walls of the building, this glass screen offers views into the garden, and then into the actual Fondation beyond. Totally transparent, the ground level of the building is clearly intended for art, but its height and light levels have posed substantial problems for many of the artists who have exhibited there. In architectural terms however, the Fondation building is a formidable success, playing on different levels of transparency and on reflections in ways that vary with each day of the year and every hour. In the upper office levels of the building, Nouvel uses a partially translucid glass that heightens the sophisticated play of light and space that he initiates at the ground level. In this, he attains a level of perfection that might be compared to the work of the American artist Dan Graham. Within the Cartier offices, Nouvel's control of the space is heightened by the use of furniture designed by the architect. His extremely thin tables succeed in creating an impression of material warmth despite the inherent coldness of silver metal. In what could have been a perfectly banal office-type building, Nouvel plays with light and space in a way that shows his awareness of art, but also of the unused potential of modern materials in architecture. The Fondation Cartier is a masterpiece, but it is not without faults. The perhaps excessive height and transparency of the main exhibition galleries has already been noted, but the bland underground galleries are evidence of an opposite error—a lack of architectural distinction for spaces intended for the finest of contemporary art. Of course curators have long revered the "white box" pioneered by MoMA in New York, but one might have expected Nouvel to do somewhat better in the underground level of this otherwise excellent building.

Two buildings completed by Nouvel in 1995, though very different in nature, were both intended for retail sales. The Euralille complex, conceived by Rem Koolhaas in the misguided theory that the arrival of the TGV in this northern French city meant that it had to attain an exceptional degree of urban density. Centered on the new TGV station designed by Jean-Marie Duthilleul, Euralille features a tower by Christian de Portzamparc, nicknamed the "ski boot" by local critics, and a very large convention center by Koolhaas (the Grand Palais). Jean Nouvel's part in the project was the external design of the vast, 92 000-square-meter shopping area and the attached residences, school, hotel, concert hall, and "World Trade Center." Rather than a full control of this space, Nouvel was called on essentially to create the external envelope that groups the facilities. Interestingly, he has again opted for what could be described as a maritime theme—with an enormous curving roof and tower sticking up through the roof like smokestacks. Though he designed more of the interior space in Tours than here, the Euralille project again demonstrates his ability to create a sophisticated and sleek exterior that groups rather disparate and complex interior functions. In this respect, Jean Nouvel was a perfect choice for Koolhaas, who was seeking to create a layered, dense urban fabric in what is otherwise a rather depressing 19th-century city.

With a usable floor area of 39 000 square meters, the Galeries Lafayette building in Berlin is just over a third of the size of Nouvel's part of Euralille, but it is certainly a more sophisticated and complete work than the shopping center. Located on the corner of Friedrichstrasse and Französische Strasse, the Galeries Lafayette is notable because Jean Nouvel managed to escape the very strict urban rules imposed on other architects for the "new" Berlin. Masonry façades and small windows are the rule elsewhere, but here a sweeping glass façade breaks the otherwise monotonous parade of recently completed structures. The rounded edge of the complex is another departure from the usually more angular Berlin street corners. The Berlin building also boasts one of Jean Nouvel's more successful attempts to bring a sense of vertiginous ambiguity to his work. The soaring Tour sans fins would have risen into the clouds, almost disappearing at its summit, while the Galeries Lafayette features cone-shaped light wells and a central void. Using screen-printed glass on parts of the façade, Jean Nouvel also plays on the use and presence of the building's external envelope. With its curves and light wells, the building allows shoppers to see others moving within in a kind of ghostly way already suggested in the Fondation Cartier's upper levels. Despite his taste for ambiguity in architecture, here, as elsewhere, the architect is respectful of the requirements of the client, be it in the high density of this structure or in its essentially simple layout, easy for shoppers to understand and navigate in. While other architects sought to make use of Berlin's overly strict building code only to find themselves trapped in heavy stone, Jean Nouvel again finds a radical solution that differs his work

Galeries Lafayette, Berlin, Germany, 1991– One of the first structures completed in the reconstruction program—glass combined wit the robustness of Berlin.

from that of others while still satisfying the economic logic that is at the origin of the project. Indeed, one might say that Nouvel's conscientious fulfillment of the client's requirements is what constitutes the purely architectural aspect of his work. His plays on light and space, his mixture of brutal solidity with floating lightness are elements that allow his work to achieve a high level of artistic expression.

In the midst of these successes, Jean Nouvel suffered a considerable defeat in October 1994 when French Prime Minister Édouard Balladur selected a project designed by Michel Macary and others for the "Grand Stade" football stadium over Nouvel's competition-winning entry. It was suggested, perhaps unjustifiably, that Nouvel's project that provided for movable stands would have been technically difficult to build, especially given the very tight schedule that required the 80 000-seat facility to be inaugurated early in 1998. It would be surprising in other democracies that the prime minister could select one architectural project over another—but in this instance, Jean Nouvel and his associated construction consortium Eiffage-Spie-Batignolles went to court to appeal against what appeared to be a completely arbitrary decision. The Administrative Tribunal of Paris agreed with the losers in a decision made public on December 1, 1997, while Jean Nouvel brought the case before the European Commission, which agreed that he should have won the competition. Unfortunately these legal decisions had no effect on the outcome—it was Macary's project that was built and inaugurated by French President Jacques Chirac in January 1998. Some asked if the association of Macary with the Bouygues construction company, owner of the country's top television network, TF1, might not have had something to do with Balladur's choice, but the net result of this incident was that a certain amount of time would go by before Nouvel was again given a major French government contract. He had already begun work on the Law Courts in Nantes when the Grand Stade matter came to a head, but the next job he got for the government was some years later, when he won the competition for the Museum of Arts and Civilizations in Paris.

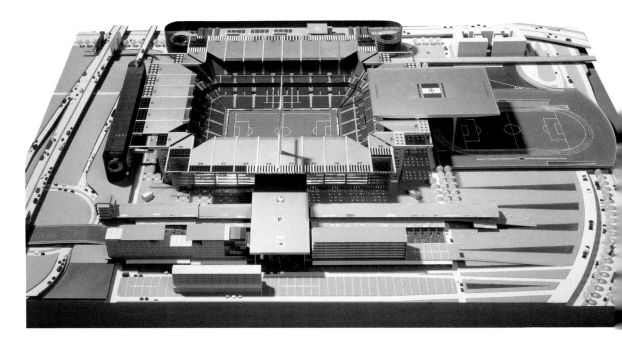

The Young Rebel Matures

Benefiting once again from an enviable site, Jean Nouvel's next major building after the completion of the Fondation Cartier was the Lucerne Culture and Congress Center, set on the shore of the lake, next to the railway station and just a short walk from the famous Kapellbrücke rebuilt after it was destroyed by fire. Intended to provide a 1900-seat symphony hall, a 900-seat multi-purpose hall, a 300-seat congress hall, a 2400-square-meter Kunsthalle, and three restaurants, the complex has a total usable floor area of 22000 square meters. Echoing the Tours Conference Center, and the Euralille shopping center in an even more spectacular way, the Lucerne Center has a surprising overhanging roof jutting 45 meters beyond the building toward the lake. Under this unifying canopy, Nouvel composes his own symphony of forms and materials, even bringing lake water into the structure with a shallow canal. Though it is next to the railway station with its entrance designed by Santiago Calatrava, the Lucerne Center is one of the most notable modern buildings in an otherwise very traditional Swiss city. Always adept at treading the fine line between respect for the past and audacious modernity, Jean Nouvel fully masters this complex and shows a maturity that may not have yet been fully developed when he designed the Cartier building. This movement toward a greater mastery of the structure may have been prompted in Lucerne by an unusual turn of events. A first proposal by Nouvel made in 1989 that would have modified the existing shores of the lake by building out into the water was rejected by a referendum, and the city asked him to propose a new scheme in 1992.

Begun in 1993, Jean Nouvel's Nantes Law Courts represent a significant commentary on the architecture of the judicial system in France. The architect here returns with a vengeance to his favorite black color scheme, paving the 113-meter-long public entrance hall of this structure with polished Zimbabwean black granite. He makes the point that justice is to be respected, especially where serious crime is concerned and

Grand Stadium, Saint-Denis, France, 1994
This flexible stadium was designed for the 19͏ Soccer World Cup and Paris's candidacy for t͏ Summer Olympic Games.

Branly Museum, Paris, France, 1999–2006
In the midst of the grand sweep of Left Bank buildings leading to the Eiffel Tower, the museum follows the curve of the Seine.

the rather forbidding appearance of the Nantes building shows just what he means. Making use of the typical courthouse typology, Jean Nouvel modifies and updates such standard features as the broad stairs and columns that grace most Neoclassical courts. A sloping cobblestone approach replaces the steps and black metal columns take the place of sandstone. Sitting on the banks of the Loire River opposite the old town of Nantes in a newly developed area, Nouvel's courthouse has all of the severity that he desired, but its soaring public spaces and view out to the river give it a degree of lightness to balance the voluntary gravitas of the design. It is to be noted that Nouvel could hardly have engaged in such a project without having his own very specific idea of justice. While others like Richard Meier in the United States have chosen to equate justice with light and clarity, Jean Nouvel takes the opposite tack, deciding that a respect for the judicial process can be imposed by a building. His revision of the Neoclassical court typology, including the generous entrance hall, is an interesting variant on his frequent pragmatic equilibrium between past and present. Typically, the Nantes Law Courts give an impression of powerful solidity.

The interest in modern art that Jean Nouvel has frequently demonstrated in his projects reached a high point with his participation in the Swiss national exhibition Expo 02 in the city of Morat. Jean Nouvel was called on to create a temporary structure on the lake. Instead, he conceived a series of interventions, the most visible of which was a monolithic block of rusting steel, sitting in the lake. Although the volume of this object was certainly more related to architecture than to sculpture, it did bring to mind the powerful Corten-steel works of Richard Serra. Another unexpected structure was an exhibition area, occupied by the Fondation Cartier and made of an enormous stack of logs. Using tents, containers, and military camouflage, Nouvel occupied Morat with his temporary designs, in a manner and style that approached installation art more than architecture. Nouvel's confidence in carrying out this commission, intentionally ephemeral, demonstrates one of the specificities of his creative approach—his close relationship to contemporary art, and his willful transgression of the usual barriers that separate architecture from less "useful" expressions of creativity. Although Nouvel's stack of logs in Morat housed a very dark exhibition area, the enormous metal block set in the lake of this attractive Swiss city had no recognizable function. It was an object in the artistic sense of the term.

Complexity and Stardom

It can be said that Jean Nouvel's career has evolved on the occasion of certain major projects. The Institut du Monde Arabe or later the Fondation Cartier in Paris mark turning points, as does the completion of the Lucerne Culture and Congress Center, his first very important foreign building. In France, architects typically specialize either in public commissions or in private (corporate) work, and very few are truly successful in obtaining work overseas. Nouvel, mixing projects like the Nantes Law Courts and the Cartier building, is an unusual case, able to handle both public and private-sector work. In his more recent projects, Jean Nouvel has continued this unusual mixture as he has branched out into more and more overseas jobs. Tokyo, New York, Rio, and Barcelona are all locations for Nouvel buildings, either completed or in the works. A real confirmation of his status as one of the most important international architects though has come again from Paris, where he was chosen to build the Quai Branly Museum on the Left Bank of the Seine, not far from the Eiffel Tower. The museum, a facility intended

for indigenous art, is a 30 000-square-meter structure set in a garden designed by the noted French landscape architect Gilles Clément. Exterior lighting here, as is the case in Barcelona for the Agbar Tower, is by Yann Kersalé. Nouvel won this project in a competition over the likes of Tadao Ando, Norman Foster, Renzo Piano, or MvRdV for a site previously promised to an international conference center because of its very central location. Though there is a glass screen near the quay and a garden within, this museum is on an altogether different scale than the Fondation Cartier. Nouvel has developed his ideas of multiple layers of transparency or reflection, and he says within, where he is also responsible for exhibition design, that his goal was to make the entire panoply of technical aspects, ranging from fire escapes to display cases, "disappear" in order to make the powerful objects visible. It might be noted that in parallel to the increasing sophistication of his projects, as evidenced for example in Lucerne, that Jean Nouvel's office has adapted a new style of computer-generated perspective that makes the designs easy to understand well before construction actually begins. This has contributed to a "popularization" of Jean Nouvel's work confirmed by a major retrospective held in 2002 at the Centre Pompidou in Paris.

As the Quai Branly Museum neared completion in Paris, Nouvel was in the process of designing two other significant cultural institutions—which will not be built. These are important because they are located outside of France and also because museums have come to represent the real consecration of international architects. Few if any other architects can claim to have designed museums on four continents and that is now the case of Jean Nouvel. The first, very surprising structure he proposed for the Museum of Human Evolution in Burgos, Spain, in 2000. The 23 400-square-meter site of this project is located on the southern bank of the Arlanzón River opposite the old city of Burgos, where a Gothic cathedral, part of the UNESCO World Heritage list, is located. The location of the former San Pablo Monastery (13th century), a military hos-

Paris Philharmonic Hall, Paris, France, 200 Jean Nouvel calls this landmark building on t edge of Paris "a gesture made by the capital **t** suburbs."

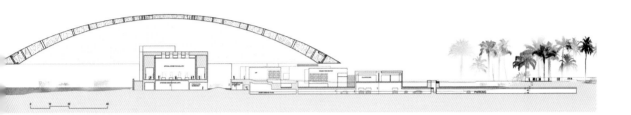

pital, and finally an army barracks, the site is considered exceptional. Burgos is also near the Atapuerca site, where numerous traces of very early human habitation have been found. In a gesture somewhat reminiscent of his Salzburg Museum competition entry, and even more so of another unbuilt project for the Guggenheim in Tokyo, Nouvel proposed nothing other than an artificial, tree-covered hill with its cave-like interior recalling the most significant local prehistoric sites. Echoing the triangular "halo" window he conceived for Salzburg, Nouvel suggested that an enormous star-shaped oculus inspired by the stained-glass windows of the Burgos Cathedral would admit natural overhead light into the interior spaces. Challenging almost every assumption about contemporary architecture, Jean Nouvel's project was a bit too radical for Burgos and he did not win the competition, but the very concept of the abandonment of walls and roofs in the traditional sense, a thought he surely had in Salzburg, here reaches an unprecedented level. The idea of dissolving or redefining the apparently necessary elements of architecture has become quite popular, as seen for example in Diller & Scofidio's Blur Building for the Swiss Expo 02 in Yverdon, but in Burgos, as elsewhere, Nouvel's thought has to do with the very specific circumstances of a given project, rather than a universally applicable theoretical stance.

And Now the World

It may be that the architectural world as a whole does not put much stock in French projects as such. Thus, the fact that Jean Nouvel has built two significant buildings on the Seine (Institut du Monde Arabe and the Quai Branly Museum) may not qualify him per se for the pantheon of the great and good, on a par with Ando, Gehry, or Koolhaas. What does, naturally, put him in that category, is that he has built (or is building) recently in such geographically dispersed locations as Spain (Agbar Tower, Barcelona, 2005, or the rather controversial extension to the Reina Sofia Museum in Madrid,

2005); Milwaukee (Guthrie Theater, 2006); or the Doha High-Rise Office Building (due to be finished shortly in the capital of Qatar on the Persian Gulf). From "old" Europe to the new Persian Gulf, the name of Nouvel has thus taken on enough clout to make him the natural choice when new and spectacular projects are envisaged. His client for the tower in Qatar is none other than the flamboyant Sheikh Saud al-Thani, member of the ruling clan of the emirate, inventor of vast cultural projects, and more recently a suspect in cases involving unusually high payments for works of art. Nouvel had also been called upon to redesign the Doha Corniche, a long stretch of largely undistinguished buildings in serious need of updating. That project, unfortunately, went the way of Sheikh Saud, even Nouvel's tower in the midst of the gulf-side drive is still rising. In case foreigners had not yet understood the significance of Jean Nouvel in the makeup of the French architectural scene, they might well ask who is being called on to design the new classical art museum in Abu Dhabi. Quite simply a local version of the Louvre, this museum is the object of a 700-million-euro deal between the emirate and the French government, providing for long-term loans and expertise to be given to one of several cultural projects planned for Saadiyat Island near the city of Abu Dhabi. The brainchild of the Director of the Solomon R. Guggenheim Foundation, Thomas Krens, who also invented the Guggenheim Bilbao with Gehry, this enormous scheme provides for new museums by not only Nouvel, but also the inevitable Ando, Gehry, and Hadid. Might it be, then, that Nouvel should be considered one of the four most noteworthy architects of the moment? Surely, but more than this, he continues to spread his reputation and his work far beyond the borders of France.

A Sense of Balance

Jean Nouvel clearly masters the functional aspects of his buildings; indeed, he has increased his mastery in this area as time has gone by. Clients know that with Nouvel they are not calling on an experimental architect who takes pleasure in shocking visitors and making them feel uncomfortable, as Peter Eisenman has claimed to do. There are moments of claustrophobia induced by some of Jean Nouvel's buildings—for example in the low, shiny black entrance foyer of the Lyon Opera—but he always balances such restricted space with much more generous and open areas. No matter how apparently extravagant the gesture, as was the case for the Tour sans fins, the architect has done his utmost to assure that technically and functionally speaking his work performs as advertised. Although his work might more readily be qualified as dark rather than luminous, Jean Nouvel frequently plays on the contrast between transparency and heavy opacity, between the bright ground floor of the Fondation Cartier and the impressive blackness of the Nantes Law Courts. Though he is surely the spiritual heir of modernism, Jean Nouvel has succeeded in defining new directions for modernity that do not necessarily reject the past. He has masterfully reinterpreted buildings—aggressively in Belfort and in a more sophisticated vein in Lyon. Nor do his modern façades shock, even in as traditional an environment as Paris. The Institut du Monde Arabe has as much claim to the status of modern classic as any other building of its time. Though he is not opposed, far from it, to ephemeral gestures—such as his rusting metal cube off the shore of Morat—his work is solid and seems thus far to resist the passage of time much better than most contemporary architecture.

Nouvel has dared to design structures that go deeply into uncharted territory, as he did in Salzburg, or more recently and in a slightly different mode, in Burgos or Tokyo.

High-Rise Office Building, Doha, Qatar, 2002–11
Geometric motifs derived from Islamic art sha[...] this tower from the fierce sun and make it sta[...] out on the already crowded Doha skyline.

r de Verre, New York, New York,
ı, 2007–
architect calls this "a structure on which to
b into the clouds."

Imagine a building that has neither roof nor façade, that looks more like a natural hill, and yet is thoroughly modern and functional. Certainly a number of eccentric architects have proposed underground or grass-covered structures, but there are few practitioners who would dare to suggest that an artificial hill covered with trees in the midst of a city could constitute a valid act of contemporary design. What is astonishing about Nouvel is the certainty of his judgment and the strength of his will. He has created unpleasant buildings, but he did so in the context of his clearly expressed ideas, of his critique of architecture. By daring to challenge deeply accepted ideas, by understanding the true relationship that can exist between art and architecture, Jean Nouvel has struck out in a direction that few have explored. In the company of some of his friends, he has occasionally put rather obtuse explanations and theories forward, but fundamentally it is his work that speaks the best of his accomplishments. Modern, functional, and, though surprising, somehow respectful of sensitive urban sites, Jean Nouvel's work is an exemplary proof that contemporary architecture can renew itself and reclaim the status of art that has often been sacrificed to material concerns in recent years. Nouvel is cautious when it comes to saying that his work is art in the fullest sense. He does little or no sketching, but rather conceives his buildings in dialogue with his clients or his collaborators. His office makes ample use of computers, but Nouvel is not one to follow the recent trends in blob-like design. He has his own direction, his own criteria, and in this, he is more of an artist than almost any other architect of his generation.

While the French may have been roundly criticized by the White House, and duly mocked by late-night talk show hosts during the time of the headlong leap into chaos in Iraq, it should be noted in conclusion that Jean Nouvel is not only an inventive individual, but also the worthy representative of a nation, France, heir to revolutionary values that did far more to promote democracy than any cruise missile, and a century that has a profound and highly self-critical culture. The fact that Jean Nouvel has thrived in this milieu might well be an indication of the significance of his rise. That he has succeeded, too, in convincing clients in Milwaukee or Doha that his vision is a correct and modern one demonstrates beyond any doubt that he is far more than a "local" figure. He is an international architect of the highest level and his sometimes "difficult" work is perfectly in tune with the times.

1980–1984 ▸ **Theater Belfort**

Belfort, France

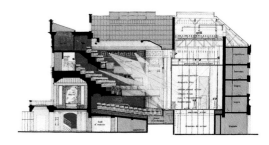

A certain number of publications about Jean Nouvel gloss quickly over his renovation of the Belfort Theater. It is almost as though commentators feel that this mixture of the old and the new does not correspond to the radical image that they associate with the architect. Actually, in the force of his intervention, and in the use of certain devices, such as the large open grid screen on the riverside, the Belfort Theater is revelatory of Nouvel's strengths. Working with François Seigneur and Jacques Le Marquet for the "scenography," Jean Nouvel chose to roughly chop into aspects of the 19th-century theater that he found mediocre and to highlight and open up the structure's qualities. The 3300-square-meter project involved two foyers, a 700-seat theater, a small 60-seat room, an exhibition area, backstage facilities, offices, and a café-bar. Harsh hatch marks signal Nouvel's exterior alterations while a layered stripping of many interior walls is reminiscent of some artistic "installation" works in abandoned buildings. Period commentary made reference to Jean Nouvel's "punk" attitude toward this renovation. Of course the word "punk" in France had somewhat less bite than in England, and the architect's roughness is compensated by a more refined attitude toward the actual theater facilities and such gestures as opening the building toward the town. There is a voluntary opposition between the "gold, lacquer, and velvet" of the theater and the "cracks, and traces of old concrete dividers running into the original walls," between a restored 19th-century carved stone façade and the diagonal hatching on poorer surfaces that were literally sawed through. Renovated and modified in an incoherent way in 1930 and 1983, the Belfort Theater was a challenge for Nouvel. Instead of trying to paper over the structure's weaknesses, he chose to leave their traces visible as he gave a new life to the building.

:
rcase appears to rise directly from a
w in the theater.

 page:
ion drawing shows the architect's play
 aesthetic of dissociation and
ulation."

ite page:
ter built in the 19th century, modified in
and renovated in 1980: exposing the
and false" strata of the building.

1981–1987 ▸ Institut du Monde Arabe

Paris, France

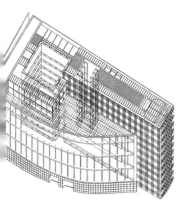

Although he carried out this project in association with Gilbert Lézénès, Pierre Soria, and Architecture Studio, the Institut du Monde Arabe remains one of Jean Nouvel's most visible and significant structures. This is, of course, due to its architecture but also to the fact that it was the first of François Mitterrand's "Grands Travaux" projects. The location, on the Left Bank of the Seine not far from Notre Dame Cathedral, means that the structure was destined to be a landmark. Intended as a tribute to the Arab world, its art and culture, the Institut has 16 912 square meters of usable floor area and was built with a budget of 341 million francs (structure). Jean Nouvel emphasizes that the building is meant to be an intermediary between the Middle East and the West but also between the old and the new. As was the case in Belfort, Nouvel worked with François Seigneur (interior architect) and Jacques Le Marquet in Paris. Winner of a prestigious Aga Khan Award for Architecture, the Institut has relatively few actual references

e:

coming through the south façade creates
mosphere likened by the architect to
ed-glass windows in the library.

site page:

imposition of surfaces and materials are
posed with each change of the outside

to Arab-Muslim design, but its south façade, opposite the Seine, deserves mention. The architects used geometric motifs derived from Islamic decorative arts to create an entire wall inspired by the *mashrabiya*. Its diaphragm-like openings were intended to open and close with varying light, but this system in fact never functioned properly. Despite this technical failure, the wall serves to bring ample but filtered light into the building and its exhibition areas. The filtering effect is indeed reminiscent of the use of light in Muslim architecture. Located near the Jardin des Plantes and the Jussieu University campus, the IMA also marks the end of the Boulevard Saint-Germain. Its long curved south wall sweeps along the quay with a studied modernity, at once integrated into the significant architecture in its environs and yet resolutely of its time.

Twenty-five thousand diaphragm-like apertures allow 30 percent of natural light to enter the building in winter and just 9 percent in summer.

Left:
A complex metallic screen plays on light and shadow, but also gives real character to the building's façades.

1985–1987 ▸ **Nemausus**

Nîmes, France

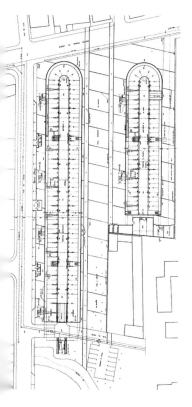

...ic plan shows the two unequal volumes
...housing complex, with their rounded
...g edges.

...rchitect calls these experimental
...ntial buildings "aluminum vessels" and
...ppearance does recall that of ships.

...ite page:
...ternal fire escape stairway with its
...rial appearance seen in a night image.

Jean Nouvel says clearly that Nemausus is his "favorite building." It is also one of his most controversial. Built when Jean Bousquet was the mayor of this southern town, it was part of an ambitious program of urban renewal featuring such architectural stars as Norman Foster (Carré d'Art). Containing 114 rent-controlled public-housing apartments, Nemausus has two distinct, ship-like volumes. The fact that they have an industrial appearance is no accident, because the architect intentionally chose to privilege the average size of the apartments (47 percent larger than average French rent-controlled housing) and to make full use of inexpensive materials. Taking into account the warm local climate, he designed all of the apartments so that they open out onto both sides of the building, allowing generous cross drafts and balconies on each side. Despite this regularity a large number of apartment types are offered, including duplex and triplex arrangements. The exterior aluminum staircases and the almost unadorned concrete walls inside the apartments are indicative of budgetary constraints, but Jean Nouvel sought to make an advantage of this limitation. Calling on François Seigneur and Daniel Buren to add touches of artistry to what might otherwise be seen as a harsh

The "prow" of one of the two nearly identical buildings with its overhanging roof and extending balconies.

Below:
Private terraces form extensions of the living areas. The façades open fully onto these terraces.

apartments are generous in size by social-
ing standards and feature full-height
ig doors that open onto the terraces.

environment, Nouvel sought to show that rent-controlled apartments were not synony-
mous with a lack of aesthetics. Built with the constant support of Jean Bousquet, Nemausus was allowed after his period as mayor to fall into a state of relative disrepair.
Elevators were not repaired, and car theft in the building's parking lot became a constant problem. Rather than allow residents to enjoy the extra space that the architect
had created in the apartments by reducing such areas as the entrance halls, the public
housing authority chose to apply a rent price per square meter, rendering the extra
space prohibitively expensive for many of the low-income residents. As a result, resi-
dent turnover has been very high and the building has been cited as a case of what not
to do in public housing. Defending his aesthetic and architectural choices, Jean Nouvel
presented an exhibition on the controversy at the 2000 Venice Architecture Biennale.
By affirming on that occasion that Nemausus remains his favorite building, Nouvel not
only underlined his own constancy but also assumed the consequences of his efforts
to improve the lot of ordinary people.

1986–1993 ▸ **Lyon Opera**

Lyon, France

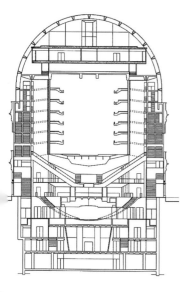

ction drawing showing the barrel vault,
actual theater with its balconies, and the
r-level spaces.

osite page:
w looking over the city hall of Lyon with
pera in the background.

Few urban projects granted to well-known architects are as well located as the Lyon Opera. Next to the city hall, across the road from the large Palais Saint-Pierre where the Musée des Beaux-Arts is located, it is a focal point of the old city. Rather than demolishing the existing 19th-century theater, Jean Nouvel chose to retain its façades and to add a bold barrel-vaulted roof. Though the scale of this effort—some 18 000 square meters of usable floor area and a construction budget of 330 million francs (1993 value)—is much larger than that of the Belfort Theater, Nouvel engages in a similar dialogue with the old building. The original building in the case of Lyon was certainly more distinguished and coherent than the one in Belfort, but Nouvel's intervention is equally bold. The barrel vault is visible from the riverside and stands out as a symbol of the cultural renewal of the city, at night as well with its red lighting. Rather than a closed metal roof that might be more typical of French urban centers, Nouvel opts here for a glass vault, emphasizing the partial transparency of the structure. Simply put, he

has in many ways succeeded in reconciling the old and the new despite an audacious approach. Surprisingly, Nouvel succeeds here in tripling the available floor space of the original theater, through the spaces below the vault used for ballet rehearsal and administration, and with large underground choral rehearsal spaces and a 200-seat amphitheater. The entrance foyer of the opera is one of its more surprising features. Black and almost ominous with its low clearances, the actual theater space appears to be suspended in the foyer. The transition to the interior allows lustrous black (a Nouvel favorite) to cede to warmer reds. This is architecture that is intended to be noticed certainly, but it also functions well as an opera. Given the rich historical environment of the Lyon Opera and its very function, it is a remarkable achievement to have also managed to create a modern building within a shell of 19th-century stone.

1989–1993 ▸ Vinci Conference Center

Tours, France

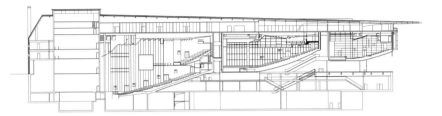

Like the Lyon Opera House, the so-called Vinci Conference Center is located in the heart of a historic town. Tours, in the Loire Valley, is of course close to Amboise, the castle where Leonardo da Vinci died. More importantly, the center is located directly across a square from the TGV railway station, where trains arrive from Paris after a one-hour high-speed run, and the prefecture offices. As Nouvel says, the challenge here was to create a building that exists in its own right as opposed to simply accompanying the architectural environment. Tours is above all an old and rather beautiful city and a major building by Jean Nouvel in its midst was not assured public approval when he won the invited competition in 1989. The large (22 000 m²) structure is distinguished from the exterior by its projecting curved roof and relatively low, beetle-like form. Built for a cost of 320 million francs (1990 value, including stage equipment), the building includes auditoriums for 2000, 700, and 350 people, an exhibition level large enough for 120 stands, 800 square meters of meeting rooms, and a restaurant large enough for 800 people. Like Lyon, the Tours building features low, shiny black public areas, with lighting coming in essentially from the glazed sides of the building during the day. At night this configuration makes the building appear to glow from within. The

ve:
ction drawing showing the auditorium
es and the overhanging cap to the right.

t:
cap of the conference center juts out over
nain boulevard of the city, opposite the
ay station and near the city hall.

osite page:
n lanterns incorporated into the
tecture offer diffracted light in the
ing.

Above:
An open view through the building in the direction of the prefecture gardens.

Right:
The architect calls this one of the "longest and most immaterial windows in 20th-century architecture."

two smaller auditoriums are suspended on cantilevered beams allowing their undersides to remain visible to the public. Jean Nouvel points out that many aspects of this building were dictated by project requirements and others specifically related to its site. Similar to a beetle in some sense or, again, to a ship, the center may surprise some by its aesthetic choices, but it is a rigorously functional building that carries with it a sense of excitement and constant activity.

1991–1995 ▸ **Galeries Lafayette**

Berlin, Germany

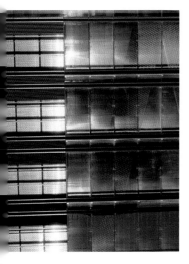

açades and their screens make
varied texture of light and shadow.

tion drawing shows the glass cones
ierce through the building, rising up
 the roof and plunging to the lowest
of the structure.

site page:
lass cones serve as pretexts to create
ions and the controlled distortion of
otions.

This large building on the corner of Friedrichstrasse and Französische Strasse combines a main space for the Galeries Lafayette department store, offices, boutiques, a small housing section, and a parking lot. The usable floor area is 39 585 square meters and the budget of the project was 211 million DM. As the architect points out, the program for this structure was particularly dense. He reacted by providing the required density but nonetheless left space for cone-shaped light wells, and, in particular, a vertiginous central void that has been the delight of architectural photographers. Jean Nouvel is one of the only architects to have escaped the draconian urban regulations of new Berlin construction that called for rigid stone façades. Nouvel points out that both Ludwig Mies van der Rohe and Erich Mendelsohn had also opposed "the necessity of designing every building in Berlin in the same manner, with brick façades, opaque walls, and little punch windows." Connected by an arcade to buildings designed by Harry Cobb of Pei, Cobb, Freed, and O. M. Ungers, the Galeries Lafayette building is an important element of the "new" Berlin. Typically, the architect has created a screen-printed glass façade that varies between a degree of transparency and a reflection of the environment. The rounded edge of the complex is another departure from

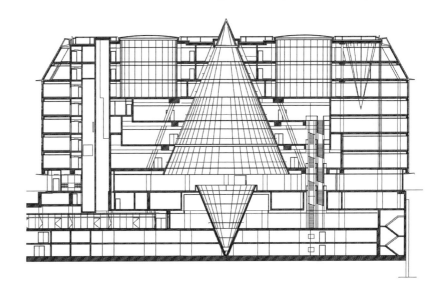

The Galeries Lafayette building is located on Friedrichstrasse in Berlin, one of the fir[...] structures to be completed in the reconstruction of the capital. The view into [...] cones is both vertiginous and kaleidoscopi[...]

A plunging view into the glass cone that forms the architectural heart of the building.

the usually more angular Berlin street corners. Here, as in many of his other buildings, Nouvel situates himself, as he has said, between the abstract and the figurative. Abstraction is found in reflections and indeterminate space such as that of the building's voids. The figurative is in the readily comprehensible open layout of the floor plans, in the overall ship-like sweep of the exterior. When he introduces an element of instability into a building, such as the plunging main cone that pierces the Galeries Lafayette, he does so in a context of an overall stability that suits the German capital. The cones that pierce otherwise solid surfaces bring light into the interiors and provide an element of orientation. This is also the case of the large open floors that obviate the difficulty that shoppers often have of finding their way in more banal and undifferentiated commercial spaces. Although there is an undeniable energy, some might even say a kind of violence, in Jean Nouvel's architecture, he compensates for his powerful originality with an affirmed capacity to make his buildings work well for their intended function. Here, as elsewhere, he creates flexible spaces that can be reconfigured for other uses with a minimum amount of work. Without making it immediately obvious, Jean Nouvel has taken on both the rigidity of the Berlin urban code and the typical architectural complacency of department-store design and has come out victorious on both accounts.

1991–1994 ▸ **Fondation Cartier**

Paris, France

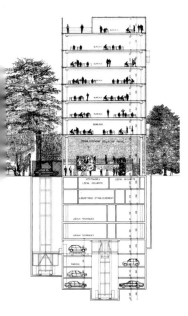

Even more than the earlier Institut du Monde Arabe, the Fondation Cartier is an emblematic building in the career of Jean Nouvel. Well located on the upper part of the Boulevard Raspail on the site of the former American Center, the most visible part of the structure is devoted to the exhibition of contemporary art. The building is surrounded by a garden, and the architect has chosen almost literally to open the ground floor out onto its surroundings. Eight-meter-high glass panes render the building

...tion shows the substantial volume of ...uilding that is located below grade.

...all glass screen opposite the front of the ...ation runs along the Boulevard Raspail ...Montparnasse.

...site page:
...ifferent layers of glass and the very ...arency of the building create a kind of ...sion born of the superimposition of ...ions.

A cedar tree planted by the French poet Chateaubriand stands in front of the entrance to the Fondation.

At sunset, or at night, the building takes on entirely different appearances, becoming ever more transparent in the dark.

almost transparent. Though this configuration has been somewhat problematic for the artists called on to exhibit in this high, entirely open space, the originality of the architecture more than compensates for these difficulties. Further exhibition spaces below grade have a more traditional "white box" layout. It is as though Jean Nouvel's recurring thoughts about degrees of transparency or opacity have reached their maturity in the Fondation Cartier. A surprising glass wall with the same enormous panes runs along the Boulevard Raspail, giving passersby a view into the garden and beyond into the Fondation itself. Depending on the light conditions, this double wall brings reflections and movement into what otherwise might have been an austere environment. There are reflections of the street, of the building itself, and of its garden. A person walking within the building is seen through this double filter and may appear to be behind a screen of greenery somehow rendered evanescent by the optics of the moment. The ambiguity thus introduced into views of the building recalls the sophisticated effects obtained by installations of the artist Dan Graham, for example. Despite its thin metallic structure, concrete floors, and omnipresent glass, the Fondation Cartier is anything but cold. It lives with its environment and is a testimony to the inventiveness of Jean Nouvel. The building includes 6500 square meters of usable floor space, 4000 square meters of which is given over to office space for Cartier S. A. The cost of the building was 98 million francs, with a further 25 million francs spent on Nouvel's interior design. Contributing to the overall impression of transparency, the elevators on the east façade use neither wires nor an exterior cage—rather they "climb" up the building.

1993–2000 ▸ **Culture and Congress Center**

Lucerne, Switzerland

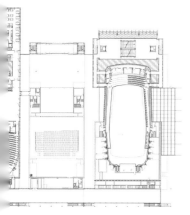

ic floor plan of the complex shows the
areas.

ark horizontal roof contrasts with the
nd distant mountains.

site page:
way into the symphony hall with a
nce of windows.

The jutting canopy of the Euralille shopping center seems like a trial run for the 45-meter overhang of the canopy of the Culture and Congress Center (KKL Luzern) in the Swiss city of Lucerne. Twenty-one meters above ground level, this canopy creates a convivial outdoor space at the lake edge and its flat aluminum panels reflect light coming from the lake. Set in a highly visible location, next to the railroad station and at the edge of the lake, this is the most important building by Jean Nouvel since his Fondation Cartier in Paris (1994). Intended to provide a 1900-seat symphony hall, a 900-seat multi-purpose hall, a 300-seat congress hall, a 2400-square-meter kunsthalle, and three restaurants, the complex has a total usable floor area of 22 000 square meters. The approximate budget for the building, whose symphony hall opened in 1998, was 200 million Swiss francs. Built in two phases in order not to disrupt the international music festival held in Lucerne, the second part of the complex, containing the multi-purpose hall, congress hall, and kunsthalle, was opened in 2000. Jean Nouvel has treated each element in a different way, the powerful black volumes of the concert hall contrasting voluntarily with the grid effect used on the façades of the museum area. A first proposal by Nouvel made in 1989 that would have modified the existing shores of the lake by building out into the water was rejected by a referendum, and the city asked him to propose a new scheme in 1992. The most stunning feature of the center remains its razor-thin roof. Its very lightness contrasts with the rather weighty volumes it cov-

Left:
Water from the lake flows through the buil[...]
in 100-meter-long canals.

Below:
The white symphony hall contrasts with th[...]
system of shadows and colors that the
architect has created around the central sp[...]

ers, but here, as elsewhere, Nouvel constantly plays on the ambiguity of weight and lightness in architecture—neither is really where it appears to be. A truly mature work, the structure is full of surprises ranging from the use of light to the astonishing materials. Another unexpected feature of the building is that Nouvel actually brings lake water inside, with long, narrow basins separating each unit of the complex. Like the roof, this gesture affirms the relationship of the building to the city and to its lake.

1993–2000 ▸ **Law Courts**

Nantes, France

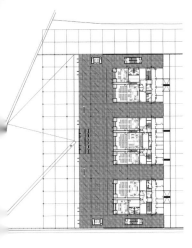

Set on a very visible site across from the old town of Nantes on the banks of the Loire River, Jean Nouvel's Law Courts are both ample and impressive. Part of a large effort to renovate the French courts that has led to buildings designed in Bordeaux by Richard Rogers, or in Grasse by Christian de Portzamparc, the Nantes structure has a usable floor area of 16 700 square meters and had a budget of 230 million French francs. A cobblestone-paved slope leads up to the high black structure, whose most prominent feature is a public entrance hall 113 meters long and 15 meters high. The highly polished Zimbabwean black granite floor reflects the sky and even the city opposite, but does not really relieve the impression of gravity or even severity wanted by Nouvel. His point, as he said clearly at the moment of the 1993 competition, was to "modernize the heritage" of judicial architecture. The large entrance hall has its origin not only in French 19th-century court architecture but also in the roots of the building typology that Jean Nouvel has sought to update. The courtrooms in Nantes are set in three 12-meter-high black cubes, whose reddish and somewhat claustrophobic interiors also speak of the significance of the judicial process. A footbridge designed by the architects Barto & Barto was added in June 2001, making the largely undeveloped site more accessible, in view of further construction, including a planned school of architecture.

The auditorium and restaurant as seen from the central square area.

1999–2005 ▸ Reina Sofia Museum Extension

Madrid, Spain

of the library. A grid is imposed on the ▮re by the architectural design.

▮on drawing shows the entire complex in ▮ to the older building.

▮te page:
▮red central square forms the new ▮ce area of the museum.

The Reina Sofia Museum is housed in the former general hospital, built in 1769 by the Italian architect Francesco Sabatini near the southern exit to the city. Nineteenth-century additions, including new wings and an extra floor, distorted the proportions of the original granite cube imagined by Sabatini. It was decided to add space to the facility at its rear where an accumulation of smaller buildings has filled existing land. Nouvel's project concerns the addition of two temporary exhibition galleries, a multimedia library, a 500-seat auditorium, a cafeteria-restaurant, administrative offices, and storage areas. He proposes a long, sloping, pierced roof in the shape of a truncated triangle covering what he calls a "chaotic" interior assemblage of the required facilities. In a spectacular atrium he includes trees and the façades of two of the earlier buildings that were located on the site. The architect suggests that this solution "brings the city into the museum" rather than the reverse. The addition was to comprise some 21500 square meters for a budget of 360 million francs at the time Nouvel won the competition in 1999. In his statement for the competition, Nouvel emphasizes the idea that the museum is annexing part of its neighborhood, but that the addition must not impose itself on the original edifice. Thus his proposal opts for a "soft, natural" approach that includes two old façades, "not because of their beauty, but to affirm the meaning of the changes." Temporary exhibitions are located on three levels with spaces intended to be flexible insofar as their space and lighting are concerned.

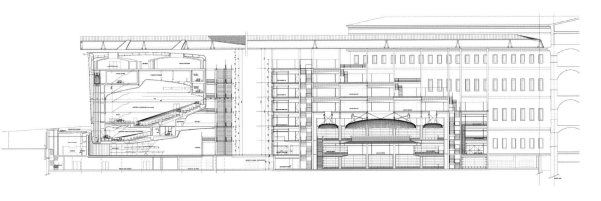

An aerial view shows the Left Bank of the Seine and the gardens in front of the muse

1999–2006 ▸ **Quai Branly Museum**

Paris, France

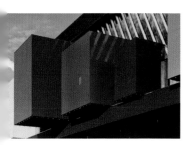

...orth façade is marked by cantilevered
...s that are made to measure for the
...ts they contain.

...:

...erall plan with the protruding galleries
...to the bottom of the drawing and the
...circulation paths in the museum visible.

...site page, bottom:
...e south façade, perforated louvers
...:t the collections. In the foreground, the
...ns designed by Gilles Clément.

As usual in France, the creation of a new museum requires the approval of government at the highest level. It was on July 29, 1998, that the French Council of Ministers announced the creation of a new institution devoted to the arts of Africa, Asia, the Pacific, and the Americas. Its collections are made up of those of the former Museum of African and Oceanic Art (20000 objects) and parts of the collections of the Musée de l'Homme (250000 objects) as well as acquisitions. Jean Nouvel was chosen at the end of 1999 to build the museum from a field including Tadao Ando, Norman Foster, Renzo Piano, and MvRdV. The museum is located on the Left Bank of the Seine River, not far from the Eiffel Tower. This was the planned site of an international conference center during the tenure of former French President François Mitterrand. As the architect says, the museum is intended to protect the works of art from harsh sunlight and yet light is a key to its design. He says that his goal was to make the entire panoply of technical aspects, ranging from fire escapes to display cases "disappear" in order to make the powerful objects visible. Working with the noted French landscape architect Gilles Clément, Nouvel created one of his most significant buildings, on the banks of the Seine. The gardens flow under and around the building in such as way as to contribute to the feeling of "disappearance" imagined by Nouvel. The complex ebb and flow of the shapes of the new museum is one of Nouvel's strongest statements in favor of a new kind of architecture: neither specifically modernist nor indeed directly linked to any other identifiable trend, it is an architecture of circumstances in the best sense of this affirmation. The building is, indeed, adapted to its collection and to its location on the Quai Branly, with the extensive garden areas imposed by the program and local regulations.

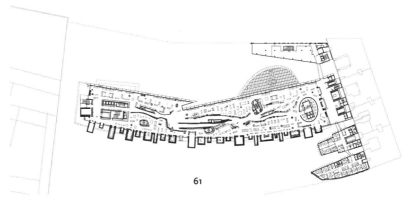

The mask gallery for Oceanic art features large showcases that "inspire dialogue and a feeling of unity amongst the objects."

Right:
The horizontal louvers that protect the works from excessive natural light are seen to the left of this image.

Work by the Australian aboriginal artist
Gulumbu Yunupingu in the hallway.

Left:
The museum seen through the gates of a
neighboring Haussmann-style apartment
building.

2000–2005 ▶ **Agbar Tower**

Barcelona, Spain

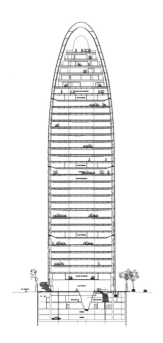

...tion shows the floor plates and areas
... grade.

...:
...gbar Tower (left) with Gaudí's Sagrada
...a visible to the right.

...site page:
...rchitect compares the effect of the
...ic grid on the building and the colors to
...uter pixels.

Whether it is seen as an airborne lozenge or a blatant phallic symbol, the Agbar Tower, set in the heart of the capital of the region of Catalonia in Spain, along the famous Diagonal Avenue, will be a reference point in the Barcelona skyline. Nouvel explains that the skin of his building evokes a rising and very substantial fountain with its many nuances of color and depth. This reference to water, as elliptical as it may seem translated from French, is a clear evocation of the client's interest since Agbar is the water company of Barcelona. The idea, in particular in this central location in the Catalan capital, is that the building should resemble a gigantic frozen fountain. It rises a height of 142 meters and has a total floor area of 47 500 square meters, including a 350-seat auditorium. Though Nouvel speaks of the liquid and thus indeterminate nature of the design, it may also evoke the rougher forms of Antoni Gaudí, such as the Sagrada Família. It also bears a partial resemblance to Nouvel's earlier Tour sans fins (Paris, 1989) because of the indeterminate nature of its façade and its strong, tubular presence. It is interesting that whether taking on relatively small-scale projects or larger, more visible ones such as the Torre Agbar, Jean Nouvel retains a sense of surprise in his designs. He rarely does what might be "expected" of him, but he can be relied upon to mark his territory while adapting his work to the requirements of the site, the client, and public expectations.

The entrance hall of the Torre Agbar with its colored patterns, reflections, and the "haziness" desired by the architect.

Right:
A view looking up to the spectacular cupola of the building.

e:
exture of the tower is generated by a
e façade that allows windows to open
leaning platforms to be installed.

rtist Yann Kersalé participated in creating
ghting system of the tower.

2001–2006 ▸ **Guthrie Theater**

Minneapolis, Minnesota, USA

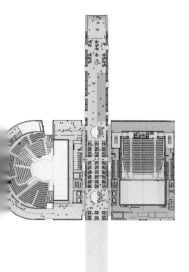

n of the theater showing the thrust
er to the left and the proscenium theater
e right.

roscenium theater where the architect
ses a powerful frontal, red design.

site page:
rchitect used "autumn colors" in this
rpretation of the thrust theater.

The Guthrie Theater opened on May 7, 1963, with a production of Hamlet directed by Sir Tyrone Guthrie, the theater's founder. The new Guthrie Theater is a 15500-square-meter theater center located in the historic Mills District on the banks of the Mississippi River in downtown Minneapolis. The project, completed in 2006, includes three theaters, offices, production and rehearsal support spaces, educational classrooms, and a restaurant. The project budget was $95.6 million and includes a 1100-seat thrust theater, a 700-seat proscenium theater adaptable to regional, national, and international productions, and a studio or experimental theater with 250 seats. The site adjacent to the Mississippi offers dramatic views down into the St. Anthony Falls, the Stone Arch Bridge, and the Mill Ruins Park from the upper levels. Connecting the audiences to these views by raising the public lobbies above the ground level became a key design goal. According to Jean Nouvel: "The exterior of the building is a composition of metals and glass that evokes industrial forms, rendered in a modern way. Given the strong association with the historical mill buildings in the massing of the Guthrie, the coloration of the building has evolved toward a dark blue color, intended to convey a jewel-like quality and the modern spirit of the Guthrie on the river within this historical context. At night, the dark blue background will recede into the sky and the graphics will appear to float in the darkness. Windows are placed behind perforated areas to frame views from within. This effect will create a dynamic quality that changes between day and night and depending on the operations of the theaters."

The architect has used a dark-blue color fo[r]
exterior. The theater foyer juts out over th[e]
site, inviting spectators to take views of th[e]
city.

Below:
Framed views contrasting with dark interi[or]
spaces are augmented through the use of
mirrors.

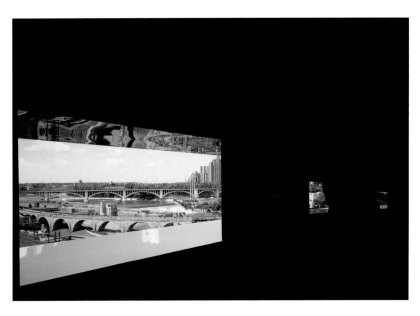

s night view, the theater is assimilated
s industrial background.

er image of the views framed by Jean
l, again with the use of mirrors inside
ilding.

2002–2009 ▸ **DR Concert Hall**

Copenhagen, Denmark

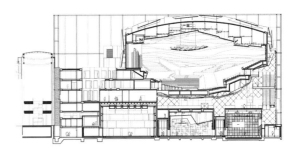

In March 2002, the Danish Broadcasting Corporation announced that Jean Nouvel was the winner of the international competition for their new 1600-seat concert hall. The 21000-square-meter complex, part of the network's new headquarters in Copenhagen, includes all facilities for the corporation's music production. Other participants in the competition included Rafael Moneo, Snøhetta from Norway, Arata Isozaki, Henning Larsen, and Schmidt, Hammer & Lassen from Denmark, and Rafael Viñoly. In June 1999 the Danish Broadcasting Corporation decided to group all of its facilities at one address in "Ørestad," the developing area on the shores of the Øresund Sound between Denmark and Sweden. As Nouvel pointed out, the unknown nature of the future surroundings of the complex complicated his task greatly. He describes his proposal as "mysterious" because its appearance would change with differing lights and numerous activities laid out along an indoor street following an urban canal. The audience arrives along this canal street, and from there goes up to the foyer levels. The upper level is placed below the "belly" of the concert hall, which hovers 10 meters above the entrance level. This configuration recalls Nouvel's earlier designs in Tours, Lyon, and Lucerne. The lower foyer is set four meters below the canal street. The architect admits here to a "discreet homage" to Hans Scharoun and his Berlin Philharmonic. Jean Nouvel completes his description of the project with his own version of Friedrich von Schelling's famous dictum "Architecture in general is frozen music," adding taste and emotion to the formula.

e right:
tion drawing shows the "belly" of the
l concert hall suspended 10 meters above
ntrance.

e:
, as in other works, the architect
iments with saturated colors and
cted images.

:
oncert hall glows with an eerie blue light
s night view.

site page:
e the building, large-scale images are
ted in spaces where the darkness is
uated by colors and lights.

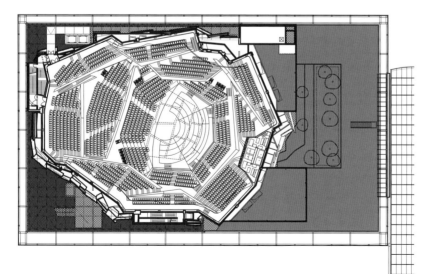

The concert hall uses a "Berlin typology" w
vineyard terraces that create an asymmetri
interior landscape.

Left:
A plan of the irregular concert hall as it is
placed within the building.

Studio 3 can be customized for any event since it has no fixed stage nor audience seating.

Bottom:
A view of the foyer into which the restaurant opens.

2005–2010 ▸ **100 11th Avenue**

New York, New York, USA

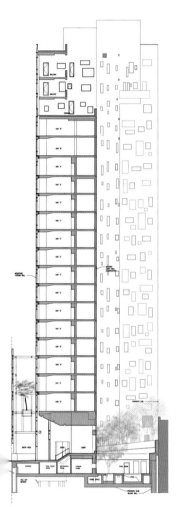

Every apartment in this residential tower has floor-to-ceiling window walls, with operable windows. Given the unusual irregular window placement in the building, each apartment also has its own unique steel window frames privileging specific views. The curving floor plan is another unusual feature of the building, commanding spectacular views of the Hudson River. The kitchens flow into open living-room areas and feature custom fixtures conceived by Jean Nouvel. Even bath fixtures were designed by the architect for Jado. The 23-story building has more than 1650 different window panes on its curved surface. Nouvel describes 100 11th as "a vision machine," with every angle and structural detail designed to create visual excitement. He writes: "On a curved surface, like an insect's eyes, facets set in different directions catch all reflections and scintillate in turn. The apartments are inside the 'eye'; they deconstruct and reconstruct this complex landscape—one shot of the horizon ... another of the white curve in the sky ... another of the boats on the Hudson River, and, on the other side, one of the midtown skyline."

...on of the building shows its tall narrow
...nd outlines the asymmetrical window
...n.

... plan shows how the tower takes
...tage of its corner site.

...ite page:
...ite buildings by Frank Gehry and
...u Ban, the tower stands out from its
...nment.

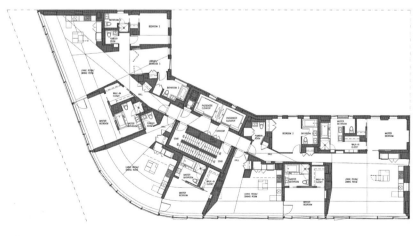

DIRECTION OF ROTATION MAP

Left Down Right Up

ANGLE OF ROTATION MAP

2°   3°   4°   5°

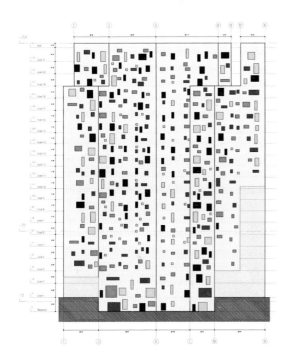

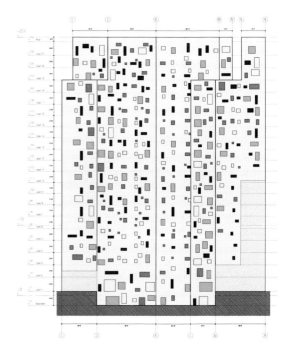

Above:
Studies of the irregular window patterns of the building. The drawings concern not only the placement of the windows, but also their angles.

Below:
Views of the building from close by, from below, and from across the street.

en from 10th Avenue, the building has a
façade that responds to neighboring
ecture.

erior view shows the irregular window
ent and framed views.

2006–2008 ▸ **The Bath by the Docks**

Le Havre, France

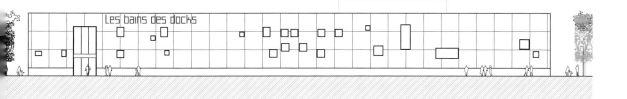

With a long history of port activity, today substantially reduced, Le Havre has undertaken a careful examination of it dockside areas, under the name Port 2000. Facilities such as the Chamber of Commerce, hotels, residences, a clinic, offices, and retail spaces are in the works for these spaces, in the hope of bringing the port back to life. A new marina for 300 to 600 private boats provided the occasion for the conversion of the Bassin de la Citadelle, where restaurants, discothèques, and cafés are installed, also to be the location for an aquatic center with a 50-meter-long exterior pool, an interior/exterior pool, and a bath therapy facility. A lobby with access to locker rooms is at ground level. Above, the pools are located near the administrative offices, a cafeteria, and a cardio-training area. Though other buildings are planned for the area, for the moment, the dark exterior volumes of the center give way to interior spaces made up of a surprising assembly of white geometric elements, a kind of interior world where water and relaxation are the rule.

:
vation shows the square grid employed
structure.

w, rectangular bath building as seen
cross the water.

ite page:
terior has numerous sculptured
es, with white dominating the bath
Nouvel's well-mastered use of
ions and colors is also in evidence.

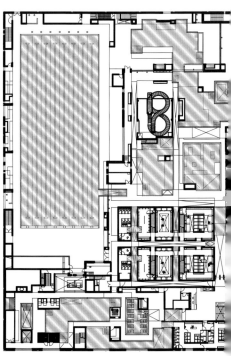

Right:
An overall plan with the outdoor pool seen to the right.

Below:
The outdoor pool area with the irregular cut-outs of the surrounding façades.

e, the baths are mostly white, with
erous unexpected spaces sculpted out of
asic grid pattern.

2009–2010 ▸ Serpentine Gallery Pavilion

London, UK

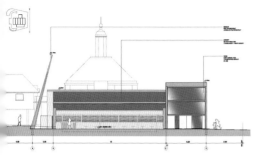

Although the land of Kensington Gardens is relatively flat, Jean Nouvel's 2010 Serpentine Summer Pavilion stood out from its green background by virtue of its 12-meter-high sloping wall but above all because of its unremitting red color. "Red," says Jean Nouvel, "is the heat of summer. It is the complementary color of green. Red is alive, piercing. Red is provocative, forbidden, visible. Red is English like a red rose, like objects in London that one has to see: a double-decker bus, an old telephone booth, transitional places where one has to go." The pavilion is bold and geometric, but then, too, with its retractable awnings and generous seating spaces, bars, red ping-pong tables, and hammocks, it is playful and inviting. Aside from the more informal daily visits of tourists, the structure was, of course, also intended for the gallery's program of public talks and events, "Park Nights." Some commentators noted that the structure might recall Bernard Tschumi's Follies at the Parc de la Villette in Paris, but Nouvel used softer materials than Tschumi did—red plastic or vast expanses of cloth. The Follies were, of course, also intended to be "permanent" structures. "His pavilion is another step into something new. A series of theatrical red planes, bars, and canopies, it stands somewhere between a hip Ibiza nightclub and Soviet constructivist agit-prop," wrote Edwin Heathcoate in the *Financial Times* (July 9, 2010). While some of Nouvel's predecessors in the Summer Pavilion series made a real point of framing the gallery's more permanent building, the Frenchman almost seemed to veil it, seeking to exist in a different continuum, though his sloping wall bowed away from the entrance path to the gallery. Although Nouvel's red certainly differentiates the structure from its environment, he spoke of its presence in more modest terms than one might expect. "I would like the Serpentine Summer Pavilion to meet with the habits of Londoners in Hyde Park, not to perturb them, to simply invite them to enjoy a complementary experience that is by no means obligatory. It would good if their curiosity were to be slightly aroused, and the desire to discover holiday feelings could spread out naturally, beginning with everyday conversations." Again, somehow obviating the structure's radical red difference from its environment, he says: "The reason the pavilion exists is to invite in the summer and the sun, and to play with them."

A view from the entrance side of the pavilion with its high angled wall on the left.

The extendable canvas cascades down to the lawns of Kensington Gardens.

Right:
A plan of the pavilion, with the Serpentine Gallery to the left.

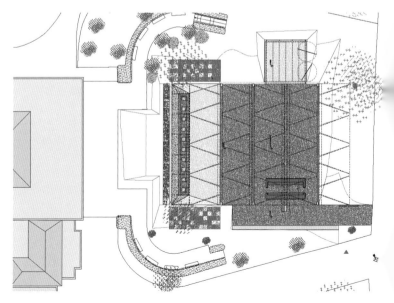

h its angled forms and insistent use of red,
pavilion stands out from the neighboring
dens and, indeed, from the Serpentine
ery itself.

ow:
der the protecting surfaces of the pavilion,
and green mix in an unusual play on
hary colors.

2004–2010 ▸ **Sofitel Vienna Stephansdom-Stilwerk**

Vienna, Austria

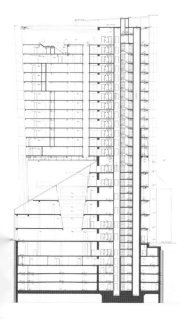

This 18-story building located near the Stephansdom includes convention and banquet spaces, 182 hotel rooms, and a panoramic restaurant on the top level. Energy saving measures concerning the heating and electrical systems cost approximately €2.6 million but are due to generate €500 000 per year in savings. The building includes spectacular backlit ceiling works by the noted Swiss artist Pipilotti Rist. "Architecture," says Jean Nouvel, "is the art of taming constraints; of poetizing contradictions; of looking differently at common and trivial things in order to reveal their singularity. Architecture is an opportunity, in a city marked by history, to continue games begun by others ... an occasion to modify, to deepen, or to change the meaning of a context." Referring specifically to this building he says: "At the limit between building and sky there is another, flat plane that reveals the appearance-disappearance of changing faces, an evocation of the multiple faces forever linked to the depth of imagery born of this city."

...tion drawing of the building shows the ...c spaces just above grade and at the top.

...ar area in the lower part of the hotel.

...site page:
...eet level, a work by the Swiss artist ...tti Rist covers the lower face of the ...evered volume.

osite page:
Sofitel seen in its urban context, standing
from neighboring buildings.

t:
staurant offering views of the city through
height glazing under a ceiling designed by
otti Rist.

w:
ew of the city under the snow from one of
ooms of the hotel.

ife and Work

Prizes and Acknowledgments

▸ born August 12, in Fumel, France.

▸ he enrolled at the École des Beaux-Arts, ...deaux; in 1966, he attended the École ...onale Supérieure des Beaux-Arts, Paris, ...ining a diploma in architecture (DPLG) in

▸ to 1970, he worked for Claude Parent ...Paul Virilio.

▸ he opened his first practice with ...çois Seigneur; from 1972 to 1984, he teamed ...n turn, with Gilbert Lezenes, Jean-François ...t, and Pierre Soria.

▸ parallel to this, he launched Jean Nouvel ...sociés, with three of his young project ...gers, the architects Emmanuel Blamont, ...Marc Ibos, and Mirto Vitart. In 1988, JNEC ...Nouvel & Emmanuel Cattani) was founded.

1994 ▸ he has collaborated with Michel ...ié within the framework of Ateliers Jean ...el (AJN).

1978 ▸ Union Internationale des Architects
Honorary Fellowship, Mexico City,
Mexico

1980 ▸ Founder and artistic director of the
Architecture Biennale, part of the Paris
Biennale

1983 ▸ Chevalier of the Order of Arts and Letters

1983 ▸ Silver medal awarded by France's
Academy of Architecture

1983 ▸ Honorary doctorate from the University
of Buenos Aires

1987 ▸ Chevalier of the Order of Merit
▸ France's National Architecture Grand Prix
▸ Silver T-square Prize for the Institut
du Monde Arabe (Best French Building
of the Year Award)

1989 ▸ Winner of the Aga Khan Prize for his
Institut du Monde Arabe

1990 ▸ Architectural Record Prize for
the Hôtel Saint James

1993 ▸ Honorary fellow, AIA Chicago
(American Institute of Architects)
▸ Silver T-square Prize for the Lyon Opera
(Best French Building of the Year Award)

1995 ▸ Honorary fellow, RIBA
(Royal Institute of British Architects)

1997 ▸ Commander of the Order of Arts
and Letters

1999 ▸ Gold medal awarded by France's
Academy of Architecture

2000 ▸ Golden Lion at the Venice Biennale

2001 ▸ Praemium Imperiale awarded by
the Japan Art Association
▸ Royal Gold Medal awarded by
the Royal Institute of British Architects
▸ Borromini Award for the Lucerne
Culture and Congress Center

2002 ▸ Honorary doctorate from the Royal
College of Art, London
▸ Honorary doctorate from the University
of Naples
▸ Chevalier of the Legion of Honor

2005 ▸ Wolf Prize
▸ Crystal Globe in the architecture
category

2006 ▸ Arnold W. Brunner Memorial Prize
in Architecture
▸ Officer of the Order of Merit
▸ Crystal Globe of Honor for the Quai
Branly Museum
▸ International Highrise Award
for the Agbar Tower

2008 ▸ The Pritzker Architecture Prize

2010 ▸ Officer of the Legion of Honor

World Map

Copenhagen
Berlin
Vienna
London
Lucerne
Paris
Le Havre
Nantes
Tours
Belfort
Lyon
Nîmes
Madrid
Barcelona

Bibliography

2006 ▸ *Area*, special issue no. 89 (Milan, Italy)

A+U, special issue 06:04 1987/2006 (Tokyo, Japan)

Jean Nouvel, Guthrie Theater / Musée du Quai Branly, Detail Japan (Tokyo, Japan)

GA, special issue no. 93 (Tokyo, Japan)

2003 ▸ *Jean Nouvel 1994-2002*, El Croquis no. 112/113 (Madrid, Spain)

Jean Nouvel, Firenze, AND (Florence, Italy)

Jean Nouvel at the Suntory Museum, catalog of the exhibition (Osaka, Japan)

Jean Nouvel at the Centro de Arquitetura e Urbanismo, catalog of the exhibition, (Rio de Janeiro, Brazil)

2002 ▸ *Jean Nouvel at the Reina Sofia Museum*, catalog of the exhibition (Madrid, Spain)

Jean Nouvel, TeNeues, Loft Publications (Barcelona, Spain)

2001 ▸ *Jean Nouvel at the Centre Georges Pompidou*, catalog of the exhibition (Paris, France)

L'inattendu Muséal selon Jean Nouvel, catalog of the exhibition Périgueux, Editions le Festin (Bordeaux, France)

L'Architecture d'Aujourd'hui, no. 237 (Paris, France)

Eglise Sainte Marie Sarlat, catalog of the exhibition, Editions Le Festin (Bordeaux, France)

AMC, Le Moniteur Architecture, special issue, December 2001 (Paris, France)

2000 ▸ *Les Objets singuliers: Architecture et philosophie*, Jean Baudrillard and Jean Nouvel, Calman-Lévy (Paris, France)

1999 ▸ *The Elements of Architecture* (French edition), Conway Lloyd Morgan, Adam Biro, editor (Paris, France)

Jean Nouvel 1987-1998, El Croquis no. 65/66 updated (Madrid, Spain)

1998 ▸ *Luzern Concert Hall*, Jean Nouvel, photographs by Jean Nouvel, Birkhauser (Basel, Switzerland)

Saper Credere in architettura-Trentuno domande a Jean Nouvel, Francesco Cirillo, Clean Edizioni (Naples, Italy)

The Elements of Architecture, Conway Lloyd Morgan, Universe Publishing (New York, USA)

1997 ▸ *Jean Nouvel*, Olivier Boissière, Editorial Gustavo Gili (Barcelona, Spain)
GA, document extra no. 7 (Tokyo, Japan)

1996 ▸ *Una lezione in Italia, Architettura e design 1976-1995*, Skira (Milan, Italy)

Jean Nouvel, Olivier Boissière, Editions Terrail (Paris, France)

The Unbuilt Jean Nouvel, 100 Projects, 3 volumes, Kenchiku Bunka (Tokyo, Japan)

Jean Nouvel, Olivier Boissière, Birkhauser (Basel, Switzerland)

1995 ▸ *Lumières*, catalog of the exhibition, Gallery-MA Books 01 (Tokyo, Japan)

Institut du Monde Arabe, Les Editions du Demi-Cercle (Paris, France)

1994 ▸ *Jean Nouvel 1987-1994*, El Croquis, no. 65/66 (Madrid, Spain)

L'Architecture d'Aujourd'hui, no. 296 (Paris, France)

Jean Nouvel, Patrice Goulet, Editions du Regard (Paris, France)

Le bateau Ivre de Jean Nouvel, Hubert Tonka, Jeanne-Marie Sens, Sens&Tonka éditeurs (Paris, France)

1992 ▸ *L'Inist dans l'œuvre de Jean Nouvel*, Olivier Boissière, Georges Fessy, Les Editions du Demi-Cercle (Paris, France)

1990 ▸ *L'œuvre récente 1987-1990*, catalog of the exhibition, Quaderns Monographies, Publications de l'Ordre des architectes Catalans (Barcelona, Spain)

Onyx. De la Vilette...de Saint-Herblain, Myrto Vitard, Clotilde and Bernard Barto, Hubert Tonka, Les Editions du Demi-Cerle (Paris, France)

1989 ▸ *Tour Sans Fins*, L'Architecture d'Aujourd'hui (Paris, France)

1988 ▸ *Institut du Monde Arabe*, Georges Fessy, Jean Nouvel, Hubert Tonka, Edition Champ Vallon (Seyssel, France)

1987 ▸ *Jean Nouvel*, Patrice Goulet, Edition Electa Moniteur (Paris, France)

Nouveau théâtre national de Tokyo, Japon, Hubert Tonka, Les Editions du Demi-Cercle (Paris, France)

1986 ▸ *Nemausus*, Hubert Tonka, Les Editions du Demi-Cercle (Paris, France)

L'Architecture d'Aujourd'hui, no. 231 (Paris, France)

Credits

Photographers and Illustrators:
Cover, 59, 60 (below), 61, 66 (above), 70 (abo 71, 72, 88-90 © Roland Halbe; 2 © Robert Doisneau; 4, 6, 17, 27, 28, 30, 38 (below), 41, 46 (below), 47, 49, 50, 52-54 (below), 55, 56 (below), 57 (left), 58, 62, 63 (above), 64-68 (below), 69, 70 (below), 73 (above), 74 (abov 75 (below), 76, 78, 79, 81, 84-87, 91 © Philipp Ruault; 7 © Albert Watson; 9-11, 18, 24, 25 © Gaston Bergeret; 12, 14 (above), 16, 26, 29, 3 34-38 (above), 39, 40, 42, 44-46 (above), 48, 54 (above), 56 (above), 57 (right) © Georges Fessy; 14 (below) © Vincent Lafont; 19, 60 (above) © Philippe Guignard/air-images.net 20 © Gaston & Septet; 32, 33 © Deidi von Schaewen; 63 (below) © Odile Fillion; 75 (above) © DR 2012; 80 © Emmanuelle Blar 82, 83 © Clement Guillaume; 92 © The Esta of Jeanloup Sieff; back cover © Peter Rigaud

The Author

Philip Jodidio studied art history and econor at Harvard, and edited *Connaissance des Arts* for over 20 years. His books include TASCH *Architecture Now!* series, and monographs c Tadao Ando, Norman Foster, Richard Meier Nouvel, and Zaha Hadid. He is internationa renowned as one of the most popular write the subject of architecture.